THOUGHTS
ON WORDS

THOUGHTS ON WORDS

BUNNY HERSCHENSOHN

BOOK DOMAIN LLC
Publish to Perfection...

All inquiries should be addressed to:

Book Domain LLC.
543 E Louise Dr Phoenix, Az 85050

Ordering Information:
Amount Deals. Special rebates are accessible on the amount bought by corporations, associations, and others. For points of interest, contact the distributor at the address above.

Printed in the United States of America.

ISBN-13   Paperback   978-1-964100-17-3
           eBook   978-1-964100-16-6

Library of Congress Control Number: 2024920053

ACKNOWLEDGEMENTS

I had "THOUGHTS ON WORDS" published because my cousin kept pushing me to do so. In a sense, SHE MADE ME DO IT. Therefore, without any reservation or hesitation, I gratefully dedicate this book to my inspiring cousin, lifetime friend and effective pusher...Jackie Hampton.

Also, I would be remiss if I did not acknowledge and give special thanks to a very special person, my guardian angel...Sonny Lee.

PRIORITIES

If you are a parent of three young children, your priorities would probably be focused on vaccinations and childhood diseases, day- care, school safety and locations, teachers, tuitions, and/or any other issues related to the educational system. If you are a senior citizen you would be more apt to focus on prescription drugs, retirement communities, Medicare and Social Security. Your priorities, *at the time*, pretty much define your politics *for that time*. I used to get excited about getting free milk at school. Now I get excited about getting a free pill cutter from anywhere. **Priorities never stay the same.**

FATE

There's one thing worse than *not* being at the right place at the right time...And that's *being* at the wrong place at the wrong time. So don't despair if you miss the boat of opportunity. Another one is on its way. **It's called destiny.**

GUILT

Since evil is guilt-free, the only people who can take the guilt trip, are good people.

FAIRNESS

Nothing is fair in life, from birth till death itself. Is it fair someone is born into wealth and security and someone else into poverty and despair? Is it fair someone is born with a gifted voice while someone else is tone deaf? Is it fair someone is born handicapped and someone else - not? Even the process to death is not fair. Is it fair someone dies in their sleep while someone else suffers and struggles to their death? Is it fair someone dies at age eighty while someone else at age eight? No, there is no fairness from birth till death and unfortunately, there is no way to equalize this unfairness except with compassion, tolerance and charity. Obviously, fairness comes after life.

GAMBLING

Gambling gives substance to fantasies, but when Lady Luck enters into the equation, all fantasies are put on hold.

MONEY

Make as much money as you want - but don't fall in love with money. Spend that love on people.

MODERATION

"EVERYTHING IN MODERATION." Imagine if Thomas Edison paid heed to this advice. Today we would be running around in the dark looking for candles instead of light bulbs. No, these words should have read, "EVERY VICE IN MODERATION." Let the creative workaholics work overtime.

DEATH

Death is not frightening dying is. It's the transition that scares people to death.

HAPPINESS

Assuming everything is relative - happiness is quite simply, *not* being unhappy. The trick is to recognize the difference between the two.

SEX AND ROMANCE

Sex is not romance. Romance is a mood.... an illusive mode... an abstract painting... a spiritual climax. Sex is reality... a demonstrative passion... an orchestrated event... a physical climax. Both are desirable.

MUSIC VIDEOS

They epitomize my worst nightmares - the ones that woke me up in a cold sweat - very creative but very scary.

JUDGMENTAL

Judgement day is **every day** for those individuals who embrace, rather than shun responsibilities. The more responsibility you have, the more you are judged. So why be a CEO when you can be a CPA? And why be a Sunday afternoon quarterback when you can be a Monday morning quarterback? Because dreamers with a purpose can't settle for less. Responsibility may invite judgement but achievement accompanied by passion and determination... trumps them both. Speaking of responsibility with incessant judgement, imagine if you are President of the United States.

PARENTS

We get different characteristics from each parent. Select only the *best* from both; ignore the rest and live accordingly with your find.

SELF DESTRUCTION

Probably, the biggest psychological problem to overcome in life is *self* destruction. Self destruction is sometimes nurtured by *guilt* that we rightfully or wrongfully, consciously or subconsciously saddle ourselves with, over a period of time.

MEEK

The dictionary defines *meek* as patient and mild, too submissive, spiritless. I have met one real meek person, to date. His name was Art Hoyt and although I knew nothing about him, I sensed and enjoyed his aura of serenity and just seeing him always brought a smile to my face. When I saw him no more, I felt a quiet loss, not for his sake, but for mine. Perhaps, the *meek should inherit* the earth.

TOMBSTONES

Tombstones are **living** proof that we are dead.

POLITICS

Politics and your *destiny* are synonymous. Case in point - When Nazism was the politics of Germany - the Jews' destiny was in the hands of the Nazi politicians.

IF

Small word...but a word for all seasons. "If" can account for all the happenings and events that take place in life... the tragedies, the happiness, the mistakes, the revelations and even futuristic dreams. The irony of this small but powerful word is, it has *no* definition...at all. "IF" can be anything you want it to be.

HUNGRY & HUNGER

We say, although we are exaggerating, "I'm dying of hunger." And, *temporarily*, that hunger-need impedes our thinking process...that is, until we eat. But, how about those people who say, "I am hungry" and that need is not fulfilled. What is their thinking process all about on a *permanent* basis?

TIME

Time is *this* moment. Yesterday's time is a memory. Tomorrow's time is a vision. Time is *this moment*.

SELFISH

If you are selfish, you're taking yourself and/or your possessions too seriously.

TRUTH

On a fat/thin scale, if half the population weighed 80 pounds and the other half weighed 180 pounds, all the *80-pound people* would be considered the *thin* ones while the **180-pound people** would be considered the fat ones. That would be truth. Same scenario. If half the population weighed 180 pounds and the other half weighed 300 pounds, now the *180-pound people* would be considered the thin ones and the *300-pound people* would be considered the fat ones. That would be truth. **EVEN TRUTH IS RELATIVE.**

ALONE & LONELINESS

Alone is the absence of people. *Loneliness* is the absence of God.

PROMISES

Promises are given too lightly and taken too seriously. If you fulfill your promises - it was expected. If you do not - you are a liar.

HUMOR

Have you ever read anything *funny* in any of the Religious Scriptures? (One exception might be when the 100-year-old Abraham and his 90-year-old wife Sarah, gave birth to Isaac. Because of their age, both Abraham and Sarah found this to be very amusing. Amusing?...Yes, but Ha-Ha funny?...I don't think so). Humor just might be man's creation and could explain why *not* everyone has a sense of humor.

VOLUNTEERS

They are the unsung heroes of the work force and the community who give an invaluable gift to society...**their time**. They ask for nothing in return and don't require an Oscar to validate their work as their rewards are of a quiet *personal* nature.

WORTHLESS

Nothing is as harmful or hateful as to tell a *person* they are *worthless*. Objects are worthless, not people.

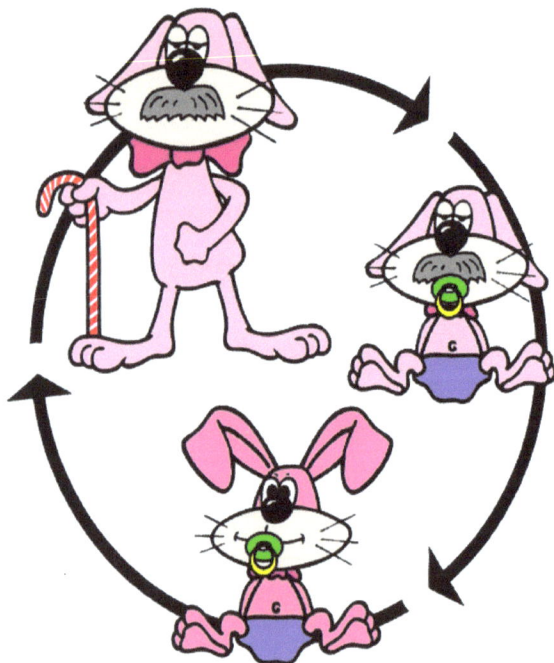

THE CIRCLE

The older we get, the younger we get. It just depends on how long we live as to how young we will become, once again. No where is this more evident than in the extraordinary similarities between babies and many, not all, of the elderly. Babies and the elderly doze off frequently during the day. Babies and the elderly have unreliable memories. Babies stagger, walk funny and fall down a lot... The elderly stagger, walk slowly and fall down a lot. Babies have no teeth... The elderly lose their teeth. Babies have little or no hair...The elderly have thinning or no hair. Babies wear Pampers...The elderly wear Depend. Babies hear but don't understand...The elderly understand but don't hear. Babies need constant care...The elderly need constant care. Observing the physical and mental effects of the passage of time is accentuated and visually captured by the very *young* and the very old. Babies are born young and re-born again... *old*. Somebody up there must like babies a lot.

NUDE AND NAKED

You never say, "I feel nude." You say, "I feel naked." Nude is the body without covering or disguise. Naked is the soul without covering or disguise.

COLLEGE

For some, college is a place to go for 4 years when you have no other place to go for 4 years.

LIBERATION

Three steps to Liberation.

- **Step one:** Identify and change the environment that eludes you of your entitled freedoms. When diplomacy is not an option, revolution is the only alternative.
- **Step two:** Follow-up on ensuring that step one is implemented and contained.
- **Step three:** Move on and away from the exclusiveness of step one and step two. Then and only then will you have absolute ... **LIBERATION**.

TOMORROW

"Tomorrow" assumes there will be a tomorrow which sub-consciously justifies our uncanny unfounded notion that we will live "forever."

REVENGE

Revenge is a present from the devil...or is it justice? You make the call...if you can.

TRUST

There are those times when we don't trust certain individuals or certain situations, but by in large, we overwhelmingly "trust" more times than not. This intangible word *"trust"* comes natural to us...like breathing. And like breathing, we don't give it much thought until something goes wrong. We trust the people who sell us our food and the place that we buy it from. We trust cars, buses, planes and trains to get us to our destinations safely. We trust elevators, amusement park rides, bridges, water, medications, buildings, etc. and people. In short we trust everyone and everything we come in contact with, everyday of our lives. That's how it is and actually, that's how it should be, lest we would become incapacitated with fear and caution. But how strange is life when such an important word as "trust" becomes a thoughtless daily routine part of living...just like breathing.

PERFECTIONIST

It's good that you care, take pride in your efforts, and want it perfect. The downside is the procrastination that might ensue trying to get it perfect. So keep an eye on **Father Time** who could precede your quest for perfection.

SWEET 16

How many SWEET 16-year-olds do you know?

COMPASSION

"I feel your pain" is a very heavy load to carry, but if you are a person who can walk in someone else's shoes, painful as it may be, you are *compassionate*. Compassion is a challenging gift from God to *special recipients* but it is probably the most GOD-LIKE attribute, you can possess.

MISTAKES

Mistakes are too time consuming to dwell upon. You are wasting today's potentially positive thinking time on a yesterday's *negative* memory.

PREJUDICE

Prejudice, in its infantile stage is an *evil thought* which, if left unchallenged or unchecked, will develop into an *evil reality*.

TRY

"Try" infers doing something you have never done before. Perhaps it's putting yourself "out there" and going out on a limb in your career or perhaps it's just making adjustments in your life style. Whatever it is...try it. They say, "You can't win them all". But if you give it a **"try"** you lower the odds on losing them all.

SANTA CLAUS

Do you believe in Santa Claus? Belief is our own personal highly individualized, revolving, evolving mind set. We don't believe what we don't *want* to believe and we do believe what we *need* to believe. As a child, an *anonymous* person left me presents on Christmas Eve. We called him "Santa Claus" and I believed in him. As an adult, I re-thought the conceptual Santa Claus-Christmas-gifts premise and concluded: people who give *anonymously* throughout the year also entitles them to be...Santa Claus. Therefore, because of this extraordinary type of giver, I *still* believe in Santa Claus.

CONSIDERATION

We usually associate consideration or inconsideration with people's words or actions, not their wearing apparel. But a **backpack** is the most inadvertent obstructive apparatus an adult, not children, can wear. Since we don't have eyes on our backs, wearing luggage on our back makes for luggage in someone else's face. Ever been on a crowded elevator with the **backpack generation**?

BIRTH & DEATH

Birth *individualizes* one person *from* another. Death *equalizes* one person to another.

HUMILITY & ARROGANCE

Humility is an honest and sincere lifetime *attitude* of gratitude...totally devoid of arrogance. Likewise, arrogance... totally devoid of humility, displays not a trace of appreciation.

DISCIPLINE

Discipline, imposed or self-imposed, brings order to your life. Without order, there is chaos. With chaos, there is instability. Consequently, a *little* discipline *can't* hurt you. A *lot* of discipline *could* hurt you. But **no** discipline **will** hurt you, in the long haul.

EMPLOYERS/EMPLOYEES

Do unto your *employees* as you would have your emplo*yers* do unto you.

PAST

If the *past* was pleasant, savor it and remember it... forever. If the *past* was *not* pleasant and you cannot rectify that unpleasantness...spit it out and erase it from your memory bank...forever.

MARRIAGES & CARS

They both break down...in time. We repair cars... why can't we repair marriages?

SHOPPING

Oprah, as usual, raises the bar even when it comes to shopping. We all do our share of shopping for others... whether it be for family, friends or an occasional stranger, but Oprah... **SHOPS FOR THE WORLD!**

ROYALTY

America's royalty appears to be entertainers, sports super-stars and the Kennedys.

4 1/2 SENSES

We taste, touch, see and smell to our fullest capabilities but on our 5th sense, *hearing*, we sometimes fall short. We hear but do we always make a conscious effort to **listen**?

GOALS

Whether your goals are major or minute, selfless or self-serving, a *goal* provides the exercise that stimulates the mind. If you have no dreams with an agenda and no initiatives for tomorrow, what is going to activate your mind today?

ABOUT THE AUTHOR

I was born in Orange, New Jersey many years ago and later moved to Hollywood, California where everyday living was like being on vacation. I now reside in Washington, DC where unlike California; vacations have a beginning and an end.

My special interests are Politics, chess, spectator football, poker and writing. As a volunteer, I worked at the White House for eight years and have worked on countless Political Campaigns. As a chess player, my claim to fame was winning the women's "American Open Chess Tournament." I am an avid Washington Redskins' fan and attribute my heart condition to their multitude of "should have won" games. And I play poker on the Internet with delusions of winning a major poker tournament. I have written and edited various projects through the years and have had a poem published.

Regarding this book, words are just words unless you give a little more thought to their meaning. Because of this goofy interest of mine, I have attempted to elaborate on ordinary words we use every day by exemplification and personalizing *said* words. Subsequently, this book is an expression of my simplistic thoughts on words with the hope there will be something in it that will apply and perhaps be beneficial to the reader.

www.ingramcontent.com/pod-product-compliance
Lightning Source LLC
Chambersburg PA
CBHW040937030426
42335CB00001B/20